A Black Man's Dilemma:
Endangered or Endeared?

Robert B. Ingram

Aglob Publishing

Aglob Publishing
Hallandale Beach, Florida
Tel: 954-456-1476
www.aglobpublishing.com

ISBN: 1-59427-021-X

Manufactured in the United States of America
5 4 3 2 1

Note From The Author

As you digest the content of this text, I pray that you appreciate the fact that it is not a statistical treatise nor is it a text about gender conflict. My focus is primarily on the transformation of the black male from the present negative stereotype to the return of our positive roles as black men contributing to our community.

Robert B. Ingram

Contents

Preface...7

Dedication..11

1. American Males: Endangered or Endeared?.........15

2. Imagery: Negative Portrayals of Black Men.........19

3. Our Own Solutions.......................................21

4. How Can We Help Our Men?..........................28

5. Taking Responsibility...................................32

6. It Is Up To Us To Help Each Other Achieve........40

Preface

As I ascended to a new level of public service having been elected to the Miami-Dade County Public School Board, the 4th largest school district in the United States, I was leaving 12 years of service as Mayor of what I affectionately called, the great City of Opa-Locka, the capital of North Dade County. Upon my reflections over the span of some 40 years, my mind traveled from the time I retired from the Miami Police department to take the position of Police Chief in the City of Opa Locka. As I cleaned out my desk and removed my name tag and reflected on my tenure with the Agency that my Godfather, John Milledge, one of the first five Black Patrol men hired by the City of Miami to patrol the streets of Miami's Colored Area, he also had the misfortune of being the first African American Police Officer to be assassinated for just doing his job.

In my packing I included a copy of a proposal that I had written to create the first "Public Service Aid", a Para-professional police program in Florida. When I finished packing and walked toward the Police parking lot I was leaving the place that I had given the past 20 years of my life in a brutal, complex history of dodging bullets, saving lives, settling disputes and challenging the system for full and equal access.

Along the way, I became the first African American police officer to be assigned to an all-white district in downtown Miami, the first African American police officer to be assigned as an investigator for a Miami-Dade County Grand Jury, the first African American to ride as a part of Miami's prestigious motorcycle unit.

As I got into my car to drive through the metal gate a sudden blast of sunlight made me take one last look at my Employment home in Miami for the past 20 years. Thinking back, I had vivid memories about many of my experiences there; saving the life of a robbery victim, helping a mother through a breached birth, quelling a situation in Coconut Grove that was escalating to riot proportions, capturing a cop killer and many other unheralded, uncelebrated, but not unrewarding, events performed during more than two decades with the Miami Police Department.

I retired from the City of Miami Police Department to become Chief of Opa Locka's police department, becoming the second African American Police Chief in the history of Miami-Dade County, Ruben Greenberg (presently Chief in Charleston) was first and Bob Ross, a veteran of Opa Locka's Police Department, once served as Interim Police Chief. Yet, I felt that nothing I would do for the rest of my life would match the turbulent, trying and triumphant days I wore the blue uniform of the Miami Police Department.

Those years solidified my passion to help move Americans generally and African American men specifically, from **Endangered To Endeared.**

Each step in my evolution from Police Officer to Police Chief, to City Manager to Mayor to School Board Member, to Professor and Pastor, has permitted me to be a part of the social change in Miami-Dade County but, more importantly, allowed me to see the problems confronting African American males and to seek ways to provide strategies for our uplift.

I pray this work, 'A Black Man's Dilemma: Endangered or Endeared," continues to help us change the social order in a positive way to uplift our brothers and sisters.

Dedication

This work grows out of my belief that if African American males knew better, we would do better. I say this having had the privilege of knowing the late Maynard Jackson. My bible, in John 15:13 notes: There is no higher calling, nor greater reward than a man who adheres to the words "Greater love hath no man than this, that a man lay down his life for his friends."

To me, there was no greater reward than having a friend like the late Maynard Jackson who personified John's instructions by putting himself on the firing line to make the promise of democracy real for African Americans, especially in times of overwhelming brutality, segregation and humiliation. That is the reason I have dedicated this work to the memory of Maynard Jackson, an African American man who stood tall in his efforts to lift our nation from the sludge of racial injustice. Maynard Jackson set a standard of excellence as the mayor of Atlanta, Georgia by waging a relentless campaign for equal opportunity where privilege and property could be equitably distributed. Maynard Jackson unashamedly used his position and power as mayor in unprecedented, but necessary and justified legal ways that created dramatic affirmative action changes for the uplift of African American people, especially African American males.

I join the thousands of African Americans and others of like mind who now celebrate the naming of the Atlanta Airport in his honor. After all, it was Maynard's steadfastness relative to inclusion of many without excluding any that led to the reshaping of Atlanta and our nation in a positive way. As you read this work titled, **"A Black Man's Dilemma: Endangered Or Endeared?"** remember it was a champion like Maynard Jackson and the power of his made-up mind that contributed to positive changes under his leadership. You see the danger in our communities is far greater than "Driving while Black". The real danger comes from not taking control over that which we have control, "ourselves." To me, Maynard Jackson was one of the most outspoken supporters of "Self-control," an offensive to not tear each other down but to lift each other up. I suggest that we build on the legacy Maynard Jackson left and as, African American males, respond to the challenges and opportunities as we go forward shaping our character to move our brothers from **Endangered To Endeared.**

JACKSON SECURITIES
INCORPORATED

MAYNARD H. JACKSON
Chairman/CEO

MEMBER
N.A.S.D
S.I.P.C
M.S.R.B
N.A.S.I
S.I.A.

12 December 1997

Ms. Michelle D. Kourouma
Executive Director
National Conference of Black Mayors, Inc.
c/o Palm Beach Airport Hilton
150 Australian Avenue
West Palm Beach, Florida   33406

Dear Michelle:

It had been my plan to speak at the 10th Annual Leadership Institute for Mayors, but a serious injury to my foot and my doctor's advice for surgery and not to make any trips for the foreseeable future have caused me to cancel coming to West Palm Beach. I deeply regret the necessity of that decision. However, Mayor Robert Ingram has been asked to make the speech and I know he will do a fine job.

All the best.

Sincerely,

Maynard

Maynard H. Jackson

MHJ:dw

100 PEACHTREE STREET, N.W. • SUITE 2250 • ATLANTA, GEORGIA 30303-1912 • (404) 522-5766 • FAX (404) 524-1552

1

American Males: Endangered or Endeared?

The question, "Endangered or Endeared?" is an appropriate one to ask about African American males. There exist some historical events that, if understood, would go a long way in correcting this problem. A look at the never-ending tragic scenes across America reveals the reasons for my concerns. For example: Remember this, Betty Shabbazz's husband, Malcolm X, was murdered, years later her daughter was arrested for plotting to kill Louis Farrakhan, and then shortly after that Dr. Betty Shabazz herself was murdered by her own grandson. All of the players were African American. Then we have Rosa Parks, the mother of the Civil Rights movement, being attacked after her home was burglarized. Her attacker? An African American, who even stated he knew who she was when he attacked her.

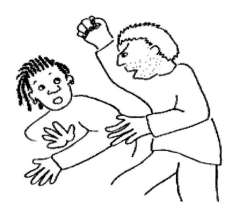

Racism is a great curse, but African American assaults on other African Americans is even a greater evil - because it provides clear and convincing evidence that the oppressed is taking on the role of their oppressors. History teaches that if there is to be progress in liberty, there must be Spiritual, Moral and Physical leadership. Clearly, Black men cannot be the kind of people that GOD wants us to be, that our community needs us to be, that our children are asking for, that our spouses want and desire until we take our rightful place in society. The issue is Black men because so many are being taken from us daily through drive-by shootings, gang-banging, drug use and abuse, and other deadly behaviors. Our rightful place in society means that, as African American men, we must be about the business of teaching and training African American people in the way of righteousness, decency, honesty, self-discipline and self-respect.

Our rightful place is not in the back of the bus. Our rightful place is up front. Not only up front, but in the driver's seat as well. For too long, following the Civil Rights Movement, too many African Americans have been satisfied sitting in the back. Now this is the characterization that the larger society has about us. Don't you find it strange that we scramble to be in the front seat at a ball game and scramble to be in the back seat of the struggle? If African Americans are to be the people we ought to be - we must take a front seat to the action. When we review the well-documented data facing our people today we see that for us, life is almost a "no-win" situation. Death, pain, sorrow and betrayal are emotions common to the Black experience.

We have no property of significance, our divorce rate is escalating, our children are killing each other, our economic condition is perilously low, and our spiritual state offers a deadly omen at best. While Corporate America is downsizing - America's Criminal Justice Corporation is upsizing. Not only that, the larger Society seems to delight in defaming black men. Coming to light after 21 years is the role of government, through groups like the State Sovereignty Commission in Mississippi, who worked hard to impede the Civil Rights movement. And Congresswoman Maxine Waters, Democrat from California, has brought to the forefront how the CIA helped to finance drugs in our Black Community contributing to maiming and killing our people.

2

Imagery – Negative Portrayals of Black Men

When one sees the continuation of the humiliation, frustration and castration of our people one cannot help but to understand, even if we must not accept, the spiraling burst of sick and demeaning behaviors. All one needs to do is to watch the 6 o'clock news to know what I'm talking about. Seems like the only time you can see us on television is when we have our hands behind our back or waving our hands in the air, and as the kids say, "waving like we just don't care," and maybe we don't care with so many of our people lying, stealing, murdering and dying.

Clearly something's wrong with us as a people and that is wrong appears to be acceptable. Why do we consistently support television programs that only show our people, especially our black men, as <u>criminals</u> or <u>comics</u>? Generally, the only time you see an African American man on television, is when we are caught acting in some sort of criminal scheme, or acting like a fool.

Martin Lawrence playing the role of Sheneneh

Oh yes, when we are on Prime Time television, most of the times we are there as crooks or comedians. Speaking of comedians, have you noticed that almost all the black comedians on television have to act like a woman to survive? Flip Wilson, as Gearldine; Martin as Sheneneh, The Waynan's (two snaps and a circle) - there is something dangerous about how Black men are characterized on television. Dangerous and injurious because we are not only observing this mess, we are absorbing this mess. It seems that for our black men to make it in this world they have to whine like a baby, act like a child and look like a girl. An unknown author has penned a verse describing the problem: *"We mutter and sputter, We fume and we spurt; We mumble and grumble, our feelings get hurt; We can't understand things, our vision grows dim, when all that we need is communion with Him!"*

20

3

Our Own Solutions

There are some vitally important issues occurring in our community that we must address. And at the top of the list, for me - is the issue of endangered Black men. What our Black men do impacts directly on the course of our community.

What is being said is this: If we have weak Black men, then we will have weak Black women. If we have weak Black men and weak Black women, then we will have weak Black children. If we have weak Black men, weak Black women and weak Black children, we will have a weak Black community. If we have weak Black men, weak Black women, weak Black children and a weak Black community, then we have a weak, wicked and warped community.

When, we, as members of the Black community, allow
our fertile minds to be inculcated with weak, obscene
thoughts, guided by weak, carnal sights, trained by
weak, cruel sounds, instructed by weak, offensive
words, directed by weak, material things, schooled in
weak, decadent places, we cannot help but produce a
weak Black people, who live wicked and warped lives.

This text is designed to solicit your help in
developing strong African American men in our
community. When I was growing up, we use to have
sweet, pretty Black women and *strong, productive Black men.*
Today, we have *sweet, pretty Black men* and *strong,
productive Black women.* Something is wrong! There is a
problem. The problem is not the *strong productive Black
women.* The problem is the *sweet, pretty, unproductive Black
men.* There was a time when we knew a woman by how
she dressed, but today the brothers have more braids
in their hair than any of the women you want to see.

22

Let me take a moment to remind you of something. The Greek and the Roman Empires, as great as they were, failed because men lost their identity. When men lose their identities and do not know what their positions are, the whole society crumbles. When we look at the statistics, we see the sisters in this community, are upwardly mobile - that is going up, and the brothers in this community are on a downward spiral.

We cannot survive with half of our community slipping down the slope of society, yielding to the magnetic attraction of worldly pleasures, caught up on the spoiled fruit of gang violence, drug trafficking, drug use, domestic violence, alcoholism, suicide and homicide. When most of the eligible Black men are being castrated by depravity that means that our women do not have anyone to hook up to, to date and to marry.

23

All is not lost, however. We can raise our sights, our goals and therefore the aspirations of our brothers, so that we can move them from ENDANGERED TO ENDEARED, for as Proverbs 28:20 says, "A faithful man will abound with blessings."

Now in order to help move our brothers to their faithful station in God's army, there are three questions we ought to ask about our brothers who are descendants of Africa. The first question is, "What is wrong with them?" The second question is, "How can he be saved?" And the third question is, "Who can save him?" So, to fully evaluate the answer of these questions, I want to parallel the condition of the Black man today with this biblical story of the *crucifixion* and *resurrection* of Jesus. I pray that you don't mind me using the Bible for that?

You see the Bible is a living testament, to learn what is right and to do what is right. Let us begin our journey by reviewing Luke 23:32 & 33, which says, *"And there were also two other malefactors led with him to be put to death. And when they were come to the place, which is called Calvary, there they crucified him and the malefactors, one on the right hand, and the other on the left."* I want to take a critical look at verse 33. *"There they crucified Him."*

"WHAT'S WRONG WITH THE BLACK MAN?" Well, one of the problems of Black men is that often times; we are being crucified both literally and figuratively. Look around; our Black men are being cast into prisons at an alarming rate. A deliberate system of castration has been set into motion that is so powerful that not only are we damned by society, and we condemn ourselves as well. BOYZ-IN-THE-HOOD and BOYS WHO WEAR HOODS (KKK) have come together as psychological contamination. Too many of our Black men are like the malefactor that said to Jesus - *"If you are so much. Save yourself."*

When we become the mirror image of those who would oppress us, that is - what they once called - when I was a boy, "FLICTED", not "A-FFLICTED" but "FLICTED". The first thing that goes into solving a problem is to recognize that you have a problem. *Is that right?* Well, the problem is, that as Black men, we are "FLICTED". When we look at ourselves and notice that we will pay $200 for a pair of sneakers but will not spend $1.00 on a tutorial program to educate our children's minds, that is "FLICTED". When we let our young boys walk around with their pants hanging down around their ankles and our girls are allowed to wear "Daisy Dukes" so short that you can see what they had for breakfast, that is "FLICTED". I've stopped by to tell you: Satan loves for you to look good on the outside and have nothing on the inside. But just like Satan can dress you up, he can mess you up. And Satan's not joking because "hell is still smoking". When it becomes socially acceptable for our young Black boys to be good at making babies but no-good at raising the babies that they make, to me that is "FLICTED". When a brother is good at profiling on the corner but his personal portfolio, that is, those things that illustrate his membership in the body of Christ, is empty, to me that is "FLICTED".

Now, one of the things that happened at Calvary was that Christ recognized how "FLICTED" Society was, and asked God to forgive them. Well, good people, we must decide if we will believe the Lord and do what HE says is right or follow the devil and do what we know is wrong. We must choose whether we will be endangered by the devil or endeared in Christ. When we put our sordid guilt in God's hands, He puts His saving grace in our hearts.

Dr. King said that the only thing necessary for evil to prevail is for good people to do nothing. So, let me hastily answer my second question: "HOW CAN THE BLACK MAN BE SAVED? I want to do this by calling your attention to the saving grace found in - Luke the 23rd Chapter and the thirty-fourth verse that says, *"Father forgive them for they know not what they do."* Now that is good news! For it tells me that whatever is wrong with the Black man, God wants to make it right. Whatever illness we have, we have a Christ chosen by God who is willing to cure our ailments.

4

How We Can Help Our Men?

"Father forgive them; for they know not what they do." Those were words that showed He, Jesus, recognized the problem. We, in the Black Community must begin to recognize our problem. How can the Black man be saved? There is no time left for play-acting and ego-tripping and all other kinds of counterfeit-behavior, we need some real answers to some real problems. We have young people going to jail everyday. Younger and younger boys and girls are being gunned down in the street everyday. And those of us whose "FLICTEDNESS" is not terminal need to open up our mouths like Philip did with the Ethiopian official: *"Phillip opened his mouth and preached Jesus to him" (Acts 8:35)*. My friends, once you know what is wrong with the brother, once you have found out that he is simply 'FLICTED' - you now need to open your mouth and get him some help. So the next question that is raised, once you know that the brother is 'FLICTED who can save him? Who can save the brother?

28

The answer can be found in the LUKE 23rd Chapter and the 55th and 56th verses, "And the women," yes, that's what is written. Verses 55 and 56 say: *"And the women also, which came with him from Galilee, followed after, and beheld the sepulcher, and how his body was laid (v-55). And they returned, and prepared spices and ointments; and rested the Sabbath day according to the commandment (v-56)."* The Bible confirms women's involvement. This testament says in a clear and convincing way that Black women must help the brothers get well. If the Black man is supposed to be all that he can be, Black Women, you are going to have to do something; sisters are going to have to prepare the spices and the ointment.

Preparing the spices and ointment is an act of faith, *Like* the old folks, Sisters, are going to have to send up some timber, for us every now and then. Sisters, you are going to have to pray for the Brothers. Now, sisters let me tell you something - I am painfully aware that the newspapers and the televisions have painted such a desperate picture of Black men that you may think that all of us are no good.

Mothers, I know that son of yours acts just like his no good, dead-beat daddy. I understand that, but you are going to have to pray for both the son and the daddy that they might get well. There is healing power in prayer. As the prayers go up, the blessings come down. I shall never forget the 43rd verse of our scripture where we find Jesus declaring to the malefactor, *"Verily I say unto thee, today shalt thou be with me in paradise"*. Even on the cross Jesus was still in the healing business. And the fact that he promised paradise to a malefactor, an outlaw, a gangster, a criminal says that Jesus still sees something good even in the least of us.

And so, what Jesus is saying to you, my dear sisters, with his words to the malfactor, **is that paradise is only a prayer away.** Hebrews' seventh chapter and twenty fifth verse says, "He always lives to make intercessions for them." O My brothers and my sisters, *'I have an Advocate above, and though I cannot see His face, I know His heart is love, and that He pleads for me'.* – Tydeman. My sisters, if you want to see this community get better, you are going to have to introduce your brothers, your husbands, your sons, your uncles and your cousins to that MAN who is still able to open up red seas.

My dear sisters, I've stopped by to tell you that we cannot give up on our Black men. Like Jesus, you can't give up. I've recorded these words to tell you that you have to be guided in the ways of that old spiritual that says: *"A charge to keep, I have a God to glorify, a never dying soul to save and fit it for the sky. To serve this present age, my calling to fulfill to all my power I will engage to do my Master's will."*

31

5

Taking Responsibility

Some of you may think that your mayor is in charge of your condition, that your governor is in charge of your condition, that your president is in charge of your condition, but I've come to remind you, that only Jesus, and Jesus alone, is in charge of your condition. It does not matter who sits in the State House or the White House, what matters is *Who* is in charge of *your* house. Jesus said, "Take my yoke upon you and learn from Me, ... and you will find rest for your souls," - Matthew 11:29.

My friends, now is the time: For shiftless folks to pep-up, for sleeping folks to wake-up, for gloomy folks to cheer-up, for crooked folks to straighten-up, for angry folks to make-up, for bitter folks to sweeten-up, for bent over folks to stand-up, and for gossiping folks to shut-up!! Oh my Dear Sisters, you must believe that God is good, even when your Black man is not. I have learned that those who know this best is those who have suffered the most.

We need a mother to sit with her son and say to him, "Son, I love you." Say to him, "Son you are somebody," and if you say it often enough he will begin to believe that he is somebody. You see the world will always tell our Black men that we are nobody. You see, even some of our mothers tells us we are nobody. Sometimes our wives say to us we are no good. Black men are so entrenched with that negative belief, that young Black men go around calling each other dogs! "My dog!" We have to stop this mess! Mothers, Sisters, Aunts, spouses and girlfriends - you need to stop the put downs, and you must stop the put downs right now if you want to save the Black man. Remember, none of us are perfect. We have all sinned and fallen short of the glory of God. Oh Sisters, if you want your daughter to marry a good Black man, then you are going to have to raise some good Black men in your household.

Stop telling that little Black boy that he is no good just like his "no good daddy". That mess needs to stop, and need to stop right now.

TELL HIM THAT HE IS LIKE *TIDE*
"He can get the dirt out that others leave behind."

TELL HIM THAT HE IS LIKE *DIAL SOAP*
"You are glad that you know him, and you wish that everybody did".

TELL HIM THAT HE IS LIKE *ALKA SELTZER*
"You tried him and you like him".

TELL HIM THAT HE IS LIKE *VO5 HAIR SPRAY*
"He can hold through any kind of weather."

TELL HIM HE IS LIKE *A PAYDAY AND A
PAYDAY "IS* BETTER THAN *NO PAYDAY."*

TELL HIM HE IS LIKE *KELLOG'S FROSTED
FLAKES "He's grrrrreat!"*

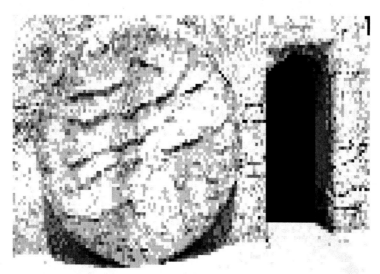

As we draw closure to this message, let us look to Luke the 24th chapter and the 2nd verse where we find Mary Magdalene and Mary the mother of James and other women that were with them seeing that the stone was rolled away, being told that Jesus was no longer in the grave: He has risen. In other words a resurrection had taken place and the man that they went looking for was not there. Now is that not good news? We can resurrect our dead Black men. When the sisters got to the grave, the only thing they saw was a grave with the stone rolled away. The only thing that they remembered is that Jesus was dead and his body was placed in a grave. But now an angel was there, the stone that sealed the grave had been rolled away, and the man that they were looking for was not there.

My dear Sisters, you are going to have to sit down with your black man every now and again, whether you are driving him to work, or driving him to school, or driving him to the movie, or driving him to the supermarket, or driving him to church. Or driving him crazy with good talk! As I mentioned before, the media only wants to show us in all kinds of negative images. But if we put forth positive images we can save our black men. You must look beyond your Black Man's faults. The God we serve looks beyond our faults. HE looks beyond our dead existence and sees black men who are potential testifiers to God's Amazing Grace. I can testify, "Amazing Grace, how sweet the sound, that saved a wretch like me. I once was lost, but now I'm found, I was blind but now I see."

Dear sisters, you must look beyond that man that you left at home. He may be a gambler, he may be a drunkard, he may be a drug abuser, he may be a domestic violator, you must look beyond that.

Because if you look beyond that, you may see a preacher, you may see a doctor, you may see a lawyer, you may see a schoolteacher, you may see some other kind of person in the service of the LORD. You cannot look at life the way you want to look at it; you must look at life the way God wants you to look at it. Our Bible says what they came looking for was not there. When you go home looking to find a dead black man, a man in the grave clothes of degradation, a man broken up by drugs, a man messed up by alcohol, a man wrapped up, tangled up, and tied in domestic violence - but that man will not be there. Somebody would have rolled the stone away, somebody would have prayed for him; somebody prayed for me! I am not what I ought to be, I am not what I prayed to be, but by the Grace of God, I'm not what I used to be, somebody prayed for me!

6

It Is Up To Us To Help Each Other Achieve

One of my favorite Bible stories is the story about Moses and the children of Israel when they fought with Amalek. The story points out that when Moses held his hand up, Israel prevailed: and when he let his hands down, Amalek prevailed (v-11). It did not take Aaron and Hur long to figure out that if Israel were to prevail over Amalek, Moses' hands would have to remain lifted up. Aaron got on one side and Hur got on the other side and stayed up Moses' hands. When Moses' hands were steady, Amalek and his people lost the battle. (Exodus 17: 10-16) My brothers and sisters, if we are to save the Black man, we have to lift him up. You may not feel like it. But lift him up. He may talk about you; but lift him up. He may not do everything right; but lift him up. He may lose his job; but lift him up. He may go to prison but lift him up. He may not make straight A's in school, but lift him up. Keep lifting the brother up. How to reach the masses, Men of every birth, for the answer Jesus gave the key - "If I be lifted up from the earth I'll draw all men unto me!"

My brothers and my sisters, the rain may fall, but keep lifting him up, the wind may blow, but keep lifting him up, the thunder may roar but keep lifting him up, and in the end you will hear the brother say: *"I was sinking deep in sin, far from the peaceful shore, Sinking to rise no more, But the Master of the sea Heard my despairing cry, From the waters lifted me, Now safe am I, Love lifted me, Love lifted me, when nothing else could help, love lifted me."* Romans Chapter 8, verse 11 says, *"But if the spirit of him that raised up Jesus from the dead dwell in you, he that raised up Christ from the dead shall also quicken your mortal bodies by his spirit that dwelleth in you."* Oh My brothers and my sisters, listen! We can save the Black man. <u>I. Chronicles 7:14</u>, says that, *"If my people, which are called by my name, shall humble themselves and pray, and seek God's face, and turn from their wicked ways; then will they hear from heaven, have their sins be forgiven, and GOD will heal their land."*

41

We can save the Black Man by following the New Testament directions found in the gospel according to <u>St. Luke 6:38</u> that says, *"Give and it shall be given unto you; good measure, pressed down, and shaken together, and running over."* We can save the Black man by finding conviction in scriptures like <u>Ecclesiastes 9:11</u> that confirms that, *" .... the race is not to the swift nor the battle to the strong, but to those who hold out until the end."* We can save the Black man using the reflective support found in <u>Psalm 37:24,</u> that says, *"I have been young and now I am old; and I have never seen the righteous forsaken; nor his seed beg bread."* We can save the Black man by finding strength in <u>Isaiah 40:31</u> that tells us: *"They that wait on the Lord shall renew their strength; they shall mount up with wings as eagles; they shall run, and not get weary; and they shall walk; and not faint."*

I've stopped by to remind you of our horrifying history. During those years: WE'VE suffered too severely; WE'VE been water-hosed too many times; WE'VE been cattle-prodded in too many instances; WE'VE been 'Billy'-clubbed by too many police officers; WE'VE cried too many tears; WE'VE marched too many miles; WE'VE prayed too many prayers; WE'VE died too many deaths; and WE'VE buried too many bodies ... Not to trust in the LORD. HE is the ONE who is able to put stars in the sky and HE is the ONE who knows every hair on your head. *HE is the ONE who can turn obstacles into opportunities.* HE is the ONE who can restore the left-out and the locked-out. HE is the ONE who can rescue the misfits and the unfits. HE is able. We find that the Psalmist authenticates, "..... *weeping may endure for the night, (Psalms 30:15), but if you do the work of the LORD there will be joy, joy in the morning!*" Let us be about God's Business and move our Black men from 'Endangered to Endeared!

Notes